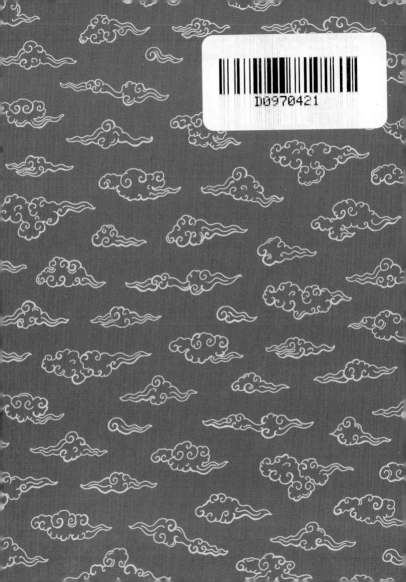

THE CHINESE HOROSCOPES LIBRARY

HORSE

KWOK MAN-HO

DORLING KINDERSLEY
LONDON • NEW YORK • STUTTGART

A DORLING KINDERSLEY BOOK

Senior Editor	🐕	Sharon Lucas
Art Editor	🐕	Camilla Fox
Managing Editor	🐕	Krystyna Mayer
Managing Art Editor	🐂	Derek Coombes
DTP Designer	🐎	Doug Miller
Production Controller	🐕	Antony Heller
US Editor	🐑	Laaren Brown

Artworks: Danuta Mayer 4, 8, 11, 17, 27, 29, 31, 33, 35;
Giuliano Fornari 21; Jane Thomson; Sarah Ponder.

Special Photography by Steve Gorton. Thank you to The British Museum, Chinese Post Office, S. G. Howlett Collection, The Powell-Cotton Museum, and The Board of Trustees of the Victoria & Albert Museum.

Additional Photography: Barrie Cash, Eric Crichton, Steve Gorton, Dave King, Stephen Oliver, Tim Ridley, Steve Shott.

Picture Credits: Bridgeman Art Library/Oriental Museum, Durham University 22cl; Bruce Coleman/Gerald Cubitt 20bl; Courtesy of The Board of Trustees of the Victoria & Albert Museum 24cr.

First American Edition, 1994
2 4 6 8 10 9 7 5 3 1

Published in the United States by Dorling Kindersley Publishing, Inc., 95 Madison Avenue, New York, New York 10016

Copyright © 1994
Dorling Kindersley Limited, London
Text copyright © 1994 ICOREC

ISBN 1-56458-603-0
Library of Congress Catalog Number 93-48006

Reproduced by GRB Editrice, Verona, Italy
Printed and bound in Hong Kong by Imago

CONTENTS

INTRODUCING CHINESE HOROSCOPES

For thousands of years, the Chinese have used their astrology and religion to establish a harmony between people and the world around them.

The exact origins of the twelve animals of Chinese astrology – the Rat, Ox, Tiger, Rabbit, Dragon, Snake, Horse, Ram, Monkey, Rooster, Dog, and Pig – remain a mystery. Nevertheless, these animals are important in Chinese astrology. They are much more than general signposts to the year and to the possible good or bad times ahead for us all. The twelve animals of Chinese astrology are considered to be a reflection of the Universe itself.

YIN AND YANG SYMBOL
White represents the female force of yin, and black represents the masculine force of yang.

YIN AND YANG

The many differences in our natures, moods, health, and fortunes reflect the wider changes within the Universe. The Chinese believe that every single thing in the Universe is held in balance by the dynamic, cosmic forces of yin and yang. Yin is feminine, watery, and cool; the force of the Moon and the rain. Yang is masculine, solid, and hot; the force of the Sun and the Earth. According to ancient Chinese belief, the concentrated essences of yin and yang became the four seasons, and the scattered essences of yin and yang became the myriad creatures that are found on Earth.

The twelve animals of Chinese astrology are all associated with either yin or yang. The forces of yin rise as Winter approaches. These forces decline with the warmth of Spring, when yang begins to assert itself. Even in the course of a normal day, yin and yang are at work, constantly changing and balancing. These forces also naturally rise and fall within us all.

Everyone has their own internal balance of yin and yang. This affects our tempers, ambitions, and health. We also respond to the changes of weather, to the environment, and to the people who surround us.

THE FIVE ELEMENTS

All that we can touch, taste, or see is divided into five basic types or elements – wood, fire, earth, gold, and water. Everything in the Universe can be linked to one of these elements.

For example, the element fire is linked to the Snake and to the Horse. This element is also linked to the color red, bitter-tasting food, the season of Summer, and the emotion of joy. The activity of these various elements indicates the fortune that may befall us.

AN INDIVIDUAL DISCOVERY

Chinese astrology can help you balance your yin and yang. It can also tell you which element you are, and the colors, tastes, parts of the body, or emotions that are linked to your particular sign. Your fortune can be prophesied according to the year, month, day, and hour in which you were born. You can identify the type of people to whom you are attracted, and the career that will suit your character. You can understand your changes of mood, your reactions to other places and to other people. In essence, you can start to discover what makes you an individual.

DIVINATION STICKS
Another ancient and popular method of Chinese fortune-telling is using special divination sticks to obtain a specific reading from prediction books.

CASTING YOUR HOROSCOPE

The Chinese calendar is based on the movement of the Moon, unlike the calendar used in the Western world, which is based on the movement of the Sun.

Before you begin to cast your Chinese horoscope, check your year of birth on the chart on pages 44 to 45. Check particularly carefully if you were born in the early months of the year. The Chinese year does not usually begin until January or February, and you might belong to the previous Chinese year. For example, if you were born in 1961 you might assume that you were born in the Year of the Ox. However, if your birthday falls before February 15 you belong to the previous Chinese year, which is the Year of the Rat.

THE SIXTY-YEAR CYCLE

The Chinese measure the passing of time by cycles of sixty years. The twelve astrological animals appear five times during the sixty-year cycle, and they appear in a slightly different form every time. For example, if you were born in 1918

you are a Horse Within the Gate, but if you were born in 1954, you are a Horse in the Clouds.

MONTHS, DAYS, AND HOURS

The twelve lunar months of the Chinese calendar do not correspond exactly with the twelve Western calendar months. This is because Chinese months are lunar, whereas Western months are solar. Chinese months are normally twenty-nine to thirty days long, and every three to four years an extra month is added to keep approximately in step with the Western year.

One Chinese hour is equal to two Western hours, and the twelve Chinese hours correspond to the twelve animal signs.

The year, month, day, and hour of birth are the keys to Chinese astrology. Once you know them, you can start to unlock your personal Chinese horoscope.

CHINESE ASTROLOGICAL WHEEL
In the center of the wheel is the yin and yang symbol. It is surrounded by the Chinese astrological character linked to each animal. The band of color indicates your element, and the outer ring reveals whether you are yin or yang.

	Water
	Earth
	Wood
	Fire

	Gold
	Yin
	Yang

· HORSE ·
MYTHS AND LEGENDS

The Jade Emperor, heaven's ruler, asked to see the Earth's twelve most interesting animals. When they arrived, he was impressed by the Horse's elegance, and awarded it seventh place.

The Horse used to represent the female in China, but in later mythology it represents the male. The Chinese language once contained many equine adjectives, but these are gradually becoming dead words. However, there are still many Chinese beliefs linked to the Horse. The white horse in Buddhist texts represents purity and loyalty; the gift of a picture of a horse and a man laden with precious goods expresses the hope for an official, well-paid position, and a picture of a monkey riding a horse expresses a hope that the recipient of the image will be given a high-ranking position.

T'ANG HORSE
This beautiful lead-glazed creature dates from China's T'ang dynasty (700–750).

THE WHITE HORSE
In the seventh century AD, the Chinese emperor sent the Buddhist monk Hsuan Chuang to India. Hsuan Chuang's quest was to find the most complete set of Buddhist scriptures, and then bring them back to China. The emperor presented Hsuan Chuang with a beautiful white horse. Hsuan Chuang was delighted with his powerful steed and rode to India. Many centuries earlier, a dragon, the son of the dragon king of the Western Sea, had been found guilty of theft and sentenced to death. Luckily, he was

THE HORSES OF MU WANG

The eight horses of Emperor Mu Wang are renowned in Chinese legend and belief and are depicted on this Ch'ing dynasty plate.

spared by Kuan Yin, the goddess of mercy. She told the dragon that in order to earn forgiveness, he must serve a monk whom she would send to him in due course.

One day, after centuries of waiting, the dragon at last saw Hsuan Chuang approach on his beautiful white horse. The dragon was quick to react. He leaped up from the deep pool that was his home and swallowed the horse whole, while Hsuan Chuang slept.

The horse came to no harm by being swallowed by the dragon. In fact quite the reverse occurred – the dragon's powers were transferred to the horse. When Hsuan Chuang awoke, he noticed nothing amiss. However, he soon discovered that his trusted white steed had mysteriously gained great powers. These included being able to leap vast distances and

becoming a brave and fearless fighter against robbers. The white horse was Hsuan Chuang's most trusted guide, but the monk was also accompanied by reprobates pardoned by Kuan Yin, such as Pigsy and Monkey.

Sixteen years later, Hsuan Chuang rode back into China, bearing the most complete set of Buddhist scriptures with him. Because the white horse had carried the holy scriptures so far and for so long, the White Horse temple was raised in commemoration of this faithful friend of humanity.

· HORSE ·
PERSONALITY

Gregarious and loyal by nature, the Horse attracts many friends, but very few will know its deeper feelings. It is extremely eloquent and blossoms in company.

You are a natural entrepreneur – inventive and superbly practical, but also fairly impulsive and impatient. The immediacy of a new idea is much more attractive to you than planning for the future. You are intuitive and can be effective and persuasive. However, sometimes you are plagued with inner doubts and tend to need plenty of reassurance.

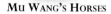

MU WANG'S HORSES
This ancient Chinese plate shows four horses of Emperor Mu Wang (1001–746BC).

same time, you need the security of recognition and personal reassurance. When you set a goal for yourself, you are immediately full of ideas and energy. However, your perseverance is limited, and when you are confronted by problems you tend to change your objective. The threat of failure causes you great anxiety, and rather than deal with the possibility of defeat, you prefer to change course, and then be

MOTIVATION
The motives behind your actions can sometimes seem to be contradictory. You need freedom to follow new interests with your characteristic enthusiasm, but at the

full of enthusiasm for the latest plan. Occasionally this personality trait works to your advantage, but you should try to keep it under control.

THE INNER HORSE

Underneath your gregarious personality is a driving desire to please and to be liked. If you feel that you are being criticized, or if you are left to fend for yourself for too long, you quickly become doubtful, withdrawn, and insecure.

You have a genuine warmth, and when you make promises you are sincere, even if they are not carried out in the way that you had planned. It is hard for you to keep secrets, and you have a tendency to become too involved in your friends' private lives. Your hot temper and ambition can make you trample those who stand in your way. This behavior is not always intentional, and often you simply find yourself being carried away by the course of events.

In your emotional life you are passionate and tempestuous, and you enjoy being swept away by the thrill and excitement of romance.

Although you may find it difficult to settle down or to make important decisions, your natural openness and love of excitement should enhance your family life.

THE HORSE CHILD

The young Horse is carefree and very affectionate. When it experiences setbacks and disappointments, it may need encouragement to persuade it to persevere.

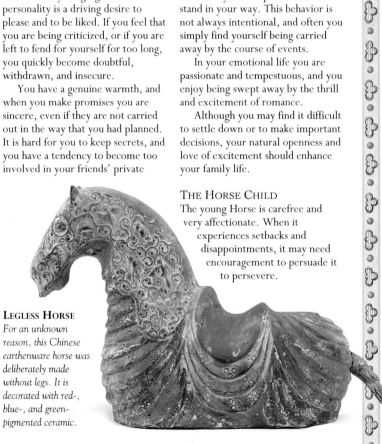

LEGLESS HORSE
For an unknown reason, this Chinese earthenware horse was deliberately made without legs. It is decorated with red-, blue-, and green-pigmented ceramic.

· HORSE ·
LOVE

The Horse is extremely passionate by nature – when it falls in love, its heart and head are quickly swept away in a tumult of exhilarating emotion.

A certain look, or a smile, can be enough to make the Horse fall in love. You are willing to abandon everything for your emotions, but this could be your downfall.

When you are overcome by your strong romantic feelings, you long for absolute involvement with your loved one. Consequently, you tend to push your job and other personal attachments aside, and this behavior may offend some people. However, your romantic nature is understood by others, and you are invariably forgiven.

In a committed relationship, try not to override your partner's decisions. You need a partner who can match your spirit, and who will allow you sufficient personal space.

Ideally, you are suited to the Dog or the Tiger. The faithful Dog will give you attention and freedom, but do not hurt its feelings. You share the Tiger's enthusiasm, and if you act selfishly it rarely notices.

Your vitality endears you to the Rabbit, but it might be too calm for

GODDESS OF LOVE
Kuan Yin is a powerful figure in Chinese mythology. Once a male Buddhist deity, she is now known as the goddess of mercy, and as Sung-tzu, the giver of children.

CHINESE COMPATIBILITY WHEEL

Find your animal sign, then look for the animals that share its background color – the Horse has a blue background and is most compatible with the Dog and the Tiger. The symbol in the center of the wheel represents double happiness.

you. The Dragon is attracted by your vivacity, but you may not pay it enough attention. The Snake enjoys the energy and variety of your moods. You are attracted by the Ram's creativity and unpredictability and by the Pig's imaginative nature, but the Pig could prove too independent for you.

The Rat and the Horse share your passionate nature. However, the Rat could become

critical of your excesses, and a relationship with another Horse could burn itself out after the initial passion has disappeared.

Relationships with the Ox, Monkey, and Rooster are likely to be troubled. The Ox is simply too sedentary and realistic for you. The quick-witted Monkey will cause you problems and is unlikely to enjoy your outbursts. Like you, the Rooster needs considerable praise, and you are likely to prove too demanding for each other.

ORCHID

In China, the orchid, or Lan Hua, is an emblem of love and beauty. It is also a fertility symbol and represents many offspring.

· HORSE ·
CAREER

The Horse is best suited to careers in which it can retain its independence. It is happiest when it has the support of a small circle of capable colleagues.

Sea horse

Chamomile

DOCTOR
Chinese herbalists use the sea horse as an ingredient in many tonic preparations. The Horse thrives in a medical career, because this gives it independence and responsibility.

Mortar and pestle

Tinctures

CHEMIST
The world of the chemist is a satisfying environment for the Horse. Here it can develop its many new ideas, inspire other people, and motivate them to carry out its plans effectively.

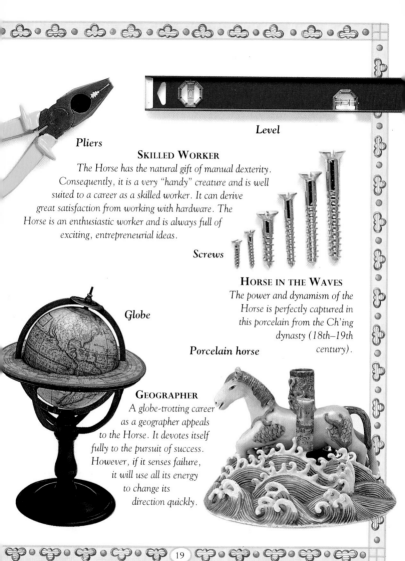

Pliers

Level

SKILLED WORKER

The Horse has the natural gift of manual dexterity. Consequently, it is a very "handy" creature and is well suited to a career as a skilled worker. It can derive great satisfaction from working with hardware. The Horse is an enthusiastic worker and is always full of exciting, entrepreneurial ideas.

Screws

HORSE IN THE WAVES

The power and dynamism of the Horse is perfectly captured in this porcelain from the Ch'ing dynasty (18th–19th century).

Globe

Porcelain horse

GEOGRAPHER

A globe-trotting career as a geographer appeals to the Horse. It devotes itself fully to the pursuit of success. However, if it senses failure, it will use all its energy to change its direction quickly.

· HORSE ·
HEALTH

Yin and yang are in a continual state of flux within the body. Good health is dependent upon the balance of yin and yang being constantly harmonious.

There is a natural minimum and maximum level of yin and yang in the human body. The body's energy is known as ch'i and is a yang force. The movement of ch'i in the human body is complemented by the movement of blood, which is a yin force. The very slightest displacement of the balance of yin or yang in the human body can quickly lead to poor health and sickness. However,

LINGCHIH FUNGUS
The fungus shown in this detail from a Ch'ing dynasty bowl is the "immortal" lingchih fungus, which symbolizes longevity.

LOTUS FLOWER
The seeds of the lotus flower are rich in vitamin C and are combined with lily to restore ch'i.

yang illness can be cured by yin treatment, and yin illness can be cured by yang treatment. Everybody has their own individual balance of yin and yang. It is likely that a hot-tempered person will have strong yang forces, and that a peaceful person will have strong yin forces. Your nature is closely identified with your health, and before Chinese medicine can be prescribed, your moods have to be carefully taken into account. A balance of joy, anger, sadness, happiness, worry, pensiveness, and fear must always be maintained. This fine balance is known as the Harmony of the Seven Sentiments.

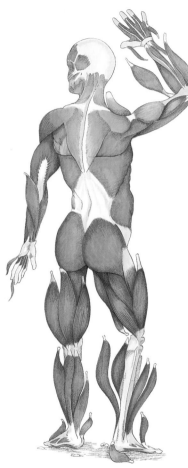

Born in the Year of the Horse, you are associated with the element fire. This element is linked with the heart, small intestine, tongue, and pulse. These are the parts of the body that are relevant to the pattern of your health. You are also associated with the emotion of joy and with bitter-tasting food.

The lotus flower (*Nelumbo nucifera*) is associated with your astrological sign. Its seeds are used to strengthen the spleen and stomach, promote mental stability, and control the loss of body fluids.

In China, lotus seed and lily soup is served at the end of wedding banquets. This is because their Chinese names form a pun on "continuous sons" and "one hundred together," and the soup represents a wish for one hundred years of married life, with many sons.

Chinese medicine is highly specific; therefore, never take lotus seeds or any other herb unless you are following professional advice from a Chinese or Western doctor.

ASTROLOGY AND ANATOMY
Your element, fire, is associated with the heart and the small intestine. The heart is a yin organ, and the small intestine is a yang organ.

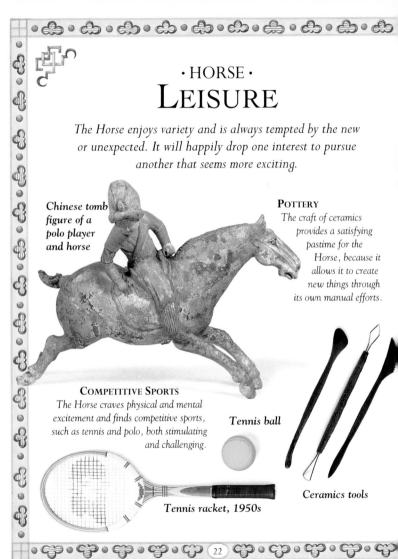

· HORSE ·
LEISURE

The Horse enjoys variety and is always tempted by the new or unexpected. It will happily drop one interest to pursue another that seems more exciting.

Chinese tomb figure of a polo player and horse

POTTERY
The craft of ceramics provides a satisfying pastime for the Horse, because it allows it to create new things through its own manual efforts.

COMPETITIVE SPORTS
The Horse craves physical and mental excitement and finds competitive sports, such as tennis and polo, both stimulating and challenging.

Tennis ball

Ceramics tools

Tennis racket, 1950s

Garden
twine

GARDENING
Manual work of any kind is satisfying
for the Horse, but it particularly enjoys
getting its hands dirty in the pursuit of
creativity. It makes an enthusiastic, if
inconsistent, gardener.

Hanging
basket

Watering can

Family
photograph,
1960s

FAMILY LIFE
The pleasures of family life are
highly appreciated by the Horse. It
likes to create a supportive family
atmosphere and will cheerfully join
the crowd for children's games.

Children's
building blocks

SYMBOLISM

Each astrological animal is linked with a certain food, direction, color, emotion, association, and symbol. The Horse is also associated with the season of Summer.

COLOR

Every Chinese New Year, small red envelopes of money are handed out to children, because red is the color of long life and good fortune. It is also the color that is associated with the Horse. This painted earthenware horse's head is from the Han dynasty (25–220AD).

Chinese earthenware horse's head

Chicory

FOOD

There are five tastes according to Chinese astrology – salty, acrid, bitter, sweet, and sour. Bitter foods, such as chicory, are linked with the Horse.

Antique Chinese compass

Hand grenades

DIRECTION

The Chinese compass points south, whereas the Western compass points north. The Horse's direction is the south.

ASSOCIATION

All forms of warfare are linked with the Horse.

Weights and spring balance

Joyful baby

SYMBOL

Weights and measures are the Horse's symbols in Chinese astrology.

EMOTION

Joy is the emotion that is connected with the Horse.

HORSE IN THE CLOUDS

~ 1954 2014 ~

This Horse can rise to extraordinary heights, as its name suggests. It is linked to flourishing and success, resulting in a very auspicious combination.

You have many of the best aspects of the Horse, such as natural diligence, determination, and loyalty. You manage to combine these qualities with an ability to rise above some of the more problematic dimensions of the Horse personality, such as impatience and a quick temper.

As long as you can control the difficult aspects of your personality, you should find yourself well favored throughout your life.

FEMALE CHARACTERISTICS

Because of the influence of the yin force, the female Horse in the Clouds may sometimes find it very difficult to control her natural tendency to speak sharply or without due care. This brusqueness should be avoided at all costs. However, if the female allows her considerate nature to take control, any problems should quickly disappear.

CAREER

Fortune is likely to smile on you throughout your life. From an early age, you should find that you have friends in influential positions. They are likely to ease the way for you, because they recognize that you are an essentially trustworthy and dependable person.

Although there may be times of considerable difficulty, you should be able to rise above them and blossom into flower when others might struggle or sink.

You are extremely lucky, because you possess an almost innate ability to take problems and solve them so successfully that they eventually turn into blessings.

FRIENDSHIPS

You are invariably known as a kind person who is loyal and faithful to friends in need and greatly valued as

Horse in the Clouds

a consequence. You are always willing to put yourself out for people – even for those whom you do not know very well.

If you find an injustice, you do not hesitate to act. This can sometimes cause its own problems, although you are usually able to transcend them, like a true Horse in the Clouds.

FAMILY

Unfortunately, you may experience various difficulties with your children, but do not worry yourself unduly. You should be able to form a very loving family, although like most Horses, you can verge toward obsession in regard to family affections and loyalty. Always try to keep these feelings about your family on a reasonable level.

PROSPECTS

As you grow older, the ever-increasing circle of friends and acquaintances who have come to value you as a true friend will invariably bring you peace and contentment. Your ability to turn adversity into happiness should ensure a happy old age.

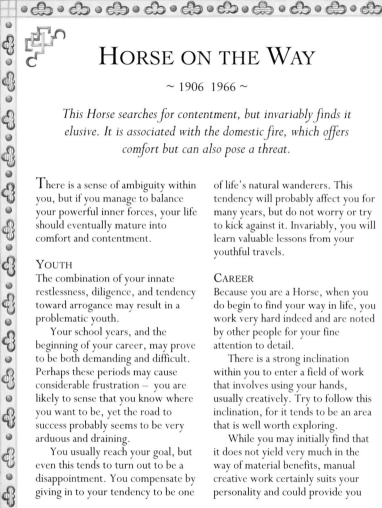

HORSE ON THE WAY

~ 1906 1966 ~

This Horse searches for contentment, but invariably finds it elusive. It is associated with the domestic fire, which offers comfort but can also pose a threat.

There is a sense of ambiguity within you, but if you manage to balance your powerful inner forces, your life should eventually mature into comfort and contentment.

YOUTH
The combination of your innate restlessness, diligence, and tendency toward arrogance may result in a problematic youth.

Your school years, and the beginning of your career, may prove to be both demanding and difficult. Perhaps these periods may cause considerable frustration — you are likely to sense that you know where you want to be, yet the road to success probably seems to be very arduous and draining.

You usually reach your goal, but even this tends to turn out to be a disappointment. You compensate by giving in to your tendency to be one of life's natural wanderers. This tendency will probably affect you for many years, but do not worry or try to kick against it. Invariably, you will learn valuable lessons from your youthful travels.

CAREER
Because you are a Horse, when you do begin to find your way in life, you work very hard indeed and are noted by other people for your fine attention to detail.

There is a strong inclination within you to enter a field of work that involves using your hands, usually creatively. Try to follow this inclination, for it tends to be an area that is well worth exploring.

While you may initially find that it does not yield very much in the way of material benefits, manual creative work certainly suits your personality and could provide you

Horse on the Way

with a comfortable income later on in your life. Try not to worry too much about the future. You always learn from your travels, and when you do settle down, you are likely to do so in the light of this wisdom.

Your financial affairs are fairly healthy – you will probably never be wealthy, but neither are you likely to be in dire financial straits.

RELATIONSHIPS
Despite the calming and soothing influence of the yin force, the female Horse on the Way can sometimes

have a tendency to provoke and engage in arguments with her partner. Sometimes these arguments can prove highly disruptive and destructive, so beware.

Unfortunately, committed relationships seem to pose problems for all Horses on the Way. These problems can be avoided to a certain degree by exercising a little thought and consideration.

Try to guard against hasty actions or statements, for these could inflame what might otherwise be just a passing period of difficulty.

HORSE WITHIN THE GATE

~ 1918 1978 ~

*Stabled, tamed, and restricted – the Horse Within the Gate
is enclosed and cannot run to the extent that nature
intended. This is not, however, a negative sign.*

You are fortunate to be associated with the ability to blossom under most circumstances. It could take some time, however, before this useful ability becomes apparent.

PERSONALITY

Always try to take the stabled Horse as your example in life. This means that you should be patient and forbearing, for there is invariably little that you can do to change your circumstances. Do not give in to listlessness and boredom.

If you are determined and concentrate on your innate Horse qualities, such as loyalty, tenacity, an adventurous spirit, and a friendly nature, this should ensure that you do not become morose.

Beware of any feelings of frustration, and try not to kick against the confines of your life. You will probably want to, for it is natural for the Horse to kick against the Gate. This will only bring you distress and discomfort, however, and you should learn to live within what you have been given, and try to make the most of it.

FRIENDSHIPS

You are kind, and although often frustrated, you usually motivate yourself to make the best of your lot. You are very generous and caring, and people find you endearing. You should enjoy many good friendships.

Your personal qualities are a tremendous gift, and you should always seek to develop them, for they are likely to have a highly beneficial effect on the lives of others, as well as on your own. Be proud of your strengths, and do not abuse them, for they should help you to bear and eventually triumph over your frustrations.

Horse Within the Gate

FAMILY

Unfortunately, you may sometimes experience severe difficulties with family life, and your relationship with your siblings can be particularly awkward and problematic.

Although it might be difficult at first, try not to be disrespectful toward members of your family, and put a little distance between you instead. This should make it possible for the whole family to enjoy a new mutual appreciation.

PROSPECTS

Sometimes you may feel that life has not always been kind to you, for it is likely that you will find yourself restricted and unable to realize your potential. Try to wait patiently, but keep yourself alert.

As you mature, you should discover ways to expand. It is likely that you will be very comfortable in your later years and will be able to reach the standard of life to which you have always aspired.

Horse in the Hall

~ 1930 1990 ~

This Horse is in an unfamiliar environment. You are associated with the hard, vital work of pounding rice and may sometimes make life more difficult for yourself.

All Horses are extremely diligent, and the Horse in the Hall is no exception. Sometimes, however, you may make more work for yourself than is strictly necessary.

Personality

All Horses in the Hall have strong personalities and are blessed with a powerful sense of compassion. Unfortunately, you may often find yourself in situations where you speak without exercising due thought, or act without pausing for suitable consideration.

This tends to happen because you are forthright by nature and do not necessarily stop to think whether your behavior is appropriate. Always try to control your naturally swift reactions, particularly if you find yourself in surprising situations or are made to feel awkward in uncomfortable positions.

Career

It is likely that you will achieve considerable success in your chosen field. If you can learn to handle the unexpected and the difficult with aplomb, then your honesty and adaptability should win you friends, as well as the admiration of people in positions of authority.

This should stand you in very good stead, for it is likely to be through the influence of your superiors that you will progress furthest in life. You should never experience difficulties in finding work, but you may sometimes run the risk of losing it if you do not successfully control your temper and your sharp tongue.

Family

You have excellent parental qualities and the fortunate ability to create a happy family atmosphere. This

Horse in the Hall

relaxed, essentially constructive environment, in which your children are given plenty of encouragement and support, is particularly beneficial to your children when they are in their infancy.

All Horses are highly committed to their families, but this admirable trait can bring problems, too. Sometimes your family may feel a little claustrophobic. These feelings can be avoided, however, if you are always aware of your children's need to flee the family nest when it is time for them to lead their own lives.

RELATIONSHIPS

In your relationship with your partner, you unfortunately have a tendency toward jealous feelings. Try to control this weakness, for it could easily sour and even destroy your relationship.

If you are always honest, but still give yourself sufficient time to reflect before committing yourself, you should be able to build a good life with your partner. With your partner's support, you can provide a secure and emotionally nourishing home for your family.

HORSE IN THE ARMY

~ 1942 2002 ~

*This Horse acts against its true peaceful spirit and involves
itself in warfare. Many demands are put upon this
hardworking Horse, and it often has to obey orders.*

It may often feel as if opposing forces
are at work within you. This could
be caused by your association with a
man carrying a pole with buckets at
each end. Symbolically, this means
that if you can remain balanced, your
life should be comfortable, but if you
lose your balance in any one area,
you could face many difficulties.

PERSONALITY
Certain elements of your nature,
such as loyalty, are overdeveloped,
whereas others, such as compassion,
may unfortunately be suppressed.

YOUTH
You are prone to mood swings. In
your youth, it may have seemed as if
you had fewer opportunities than
anyone else. You probably had to
force yourself to fit in with other
people's plans and ideas. This never
pleases you, but cannot be avoided.

You are like the conscript Horse in
the Army and will probably find
yourself under various orders.

Unfortunately, you tend to take
the majority of your frustrations out
on your family. This is completely
unfair – try to remember that your
family, and the people who are close
to you, are not there to be kicked
and hurt when you feel disappointed,
angry, or depressed.

CAREER
All Horses are hardworking, and you
always try your best. At first, you
may seem to get little reward for
your effort. It is advisable, therefore,
for you to develop your sense of
thrift quickly. This should ensure
that you survive the lean early years
of your career.

For a considerable period during
your working life, money may not be
plentiful, and you may seem static in

Horse in the Army

your professional position. Do not despair, however, and certainly never give up.

Your affairs will invariably change, and possibly quite suddenly. You are likely to find that you will eventually reap the rewards for all your years of hard work, and they may come in an unexpected or spectacular way.

PROSPECTS

In your later years, you should enjoy financial comfort, and may even find yourself rich and famous. Great wealth and riches could arrive when you least expect them, and your considerable tenacity will ensure that people will always be interested in the story of your struggle.

Because of the gentle and calming effects of the yin influence, the female Horse in the Army should be particularly prepared for a highly beneficial change of fortune during her later years.

All Horses in the Army should take time to reflect, and remember the valuable lessons they have learned from their years of thrift: always treat any increase in fortune with good sense and caution.

YOUR CHINESE MONTH OF BIRTH

Find the table with your year of birth, and see where your birthday falls. For example, if you were born on August 30, 1954, you were born in Chinese month 8.

1 You are assertive, self-centered, and aggressive. Try to appreciate your need for friendship.

2 You are popular, but can be naive. Learn to control your pride, and beware of shady financial deals.

3 You are brave and kind, and like to daydream. Try to be more realistic in your expectations.

4 You can appear to be offensive and aggressive. Curb these traits if you wish to gain authority.

5 You have good judgment and are sensible. You are passionate, but your feelings can easily fade.

6 You are successful, popular, and skillful. Try to find a business partner whom you can trust.

7 You are very honorable, and your friends are more important to you than wealth and success.

8 You allow your emotions to rule you and are rarely logical. Try to be more considerate.

9 You are honest and good company. Focus your attention when your life becomes difficult.

10 You are confident and make friends easily. Do not be too proud to ask for advice when you need it.

11 You are a natural loner and could make a good investigator. Try not to be too lazy, however.

12 You have two aspects to your personality – hardworking and generous, and cold and calculating.

* Some Chinese years contain double months:	
1906: Month 4	1930: Month 6
April 24 – May 22	June 26 – July 25
May 23 – June 21	July 26 – Aug 23
1966: Month 3	1990: Month 5
March 22 – April 20	May 24 – Jun 22
April 21 – May 19	Jun 23 – July 21

1906	
Jan 25 – Feb 22	1
Feb 23 – March 24	2
March 25 – April 23	3
*See double months box	4
June 22 – July 20	5
July 21 – Aug 19	6
Aug 20 – Sept 17	7
Sept 18 – Oct 17	8
Oct 18 – Nov 15	9
Nov 16 – Dec 15	10
Dec 16 – Jan 13 1907	11
Jan 14 – Feb 12	12

1918	
Feb 11 – March 12	1
March 13 – April 10	2
April 11 – May 9	3
May 10 – June 8	4
June 9 – July 7	5
July 8 – Aug 6	6
Aug 7 – Sept 4	7
Sept 5 – Oct 4	8
Oct 5 – Nov 3	9
Nov 4 – Dec 2	10
Dec 3 – Jan 1 1919	11
Jan 2 – Jan 31	12

1930	
Jan 30 – Feb 27	1
Feb 28 – March 29	2
March 30 – April 28	3
April 29 – May 27	4
May 28 – June 25	5
*See double months box	6
Aug 24 – Sept 21	7
Sept 22 – Oct 21	8
Oct 22 – Nov 19	9
Nov 20 – Dec 19	10
Dec 20 – Jan 18 1931	11
Jan 19 – Feb 16	12

1942	
Feb 15 – March 16	1
March 17 – April 14	2
April 15 – May 14	3
May 15 – June 13	4
June 14 – July 12	5
July 13 – Aug 11	6
Aug 12 – Sept 9	7
Sept 10 – Oct 9	8
Oct 10 – Nov 7	9
Nov 8 – Dec 7	10
Dec 8 – Jan 5 1943	11
Jan 6 – Feb 4	12

1954	
Feb 3 – March 4	1
March 5 – April 2	2
April 3 – May 2	3
May 3 – May 31	4
June 1 – June 29	5
June 30 – July 29	6
July 30 – Aug 27	7
Aug 28 – Sept 26	8
Sept 27 – Oct 26	9
Oct 27 – Nov 25	10
Nov 25 – Dec 24	11
Dec 25 – Jan 23 1955	12

1966	
Jan 21 – Feb 19	1
Feb 20 – March 21	2
*See double months box	3
May 20 – June 18	4
June 19 – July 17	5
July 18 – Aug 15	6
Aug 16 – Sept 14	7
Sept 15 – Oct 13	8
Oct 14 – Nov 11	9
Nov 12 – Dec 11	10
Dec 12 – Jan 10 1967	11
Jan 11 – Feb 8	12

1978	
Feb 7 – March 8	1
March 9 – April 6	2
April 7 – May 6	3
May 7 – June 5	4
June 6 – July 4	5
July 5 – Aug 3	6
Aug 4 – Sept 1	7
Sept 2 – Oct 1	8
Oct 2 – Oct 31	9
Nov 1 – Nov 29	10
Nov 30 – Dec 29	11
Dec 30 – Jan 27 1979	12

1990	
Jan 27 – Feb 24	1
Feb 25 – March 26	2
March 27 – April 24	3
April 25 – May 23	4
*See double months box	5
July 22 – Aug 19	6
Aug 20 – Sept 18	7
Sept 19 – Oct 17	8
Oct 18 – Nov 16	9
Nov 17 – Dec 16	10
Dec 17 – Jan 15 1991	11
Jan 16 – Feb 14	12

2002	
Feb 12 – March 13	1
March 14 – April 12	2
April 13 – May 11	3
May 12 – June 10	4
June 11 – July 9	5
July 10 – Aug 8	6
Aug 9 – Sept 6	7
Sept 7 – Oct 5	8
Oct 6 – Nov 4	9
Nov 5 – Dec 3	10
Dec 4 – Jan 2 2003	11
Jan 3 – Jan 31	12

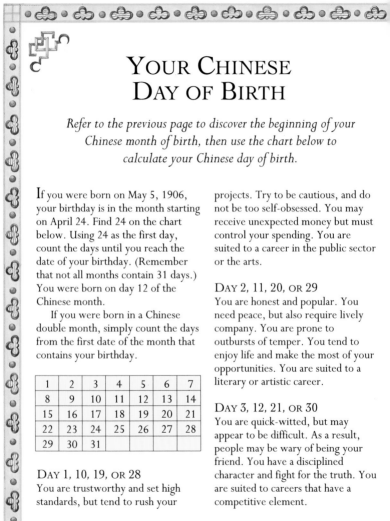

YOUR CHINESE
DAY OF BIRTH

Refer to the previous page to discover the beginning of your Chinese month of birth, then use the chart below to calculate your Chinese day of birth.

If you were born on May 5, 1906, your birthday is in the month starting on April 24. Find 24 on the chart below. Using 24 as the first day, count the days until you reach the date of your birthday. (Remember that not all months contain 31 days.) You were born on day 12 of the Chinese month.

If you were born in a Chinese double month, simply count the days from the first date of the month that contains your birthday.

1	2	3	4	5	6	7
8	9	10	11	12	13	14
15	16	17	18	19	20	21
22	23	24	25	26	27	28
29	30	31				

DAY 1, 10, 19, OR 28
You are trustworthy and set high standards, but tend to rush your projects. Try to be cautious, and do not be too self-obsessed. You may receive unexpected money but must control your spending. You are suited to a career in the public sector or the arts.

DAY 2, 11, 20, OR 29
You are honest and popular. You need peace, but also require lively company. You are prone to outbursts of temper. You tend to enjoy life and make the most of your opportunities. You are suited to a literary or artistic career.

DAY 3, 12, 21, OR 30
You are quick-witted, but may appear to be difficult. As a result, people may be wary of being your friend. You have a disciplined character and fight for the truth. You are suited to careers that have a competitive element.

Day 4, 13, 22, or 31

You are very warmhearted, but also have a reserved attitude, which can sometimes make you appear unapproachable. If you try to be more outgoing and sociable, you should become more popular. You have a calm and patient manner, and are suited to a career as an academic or researcher.

Day 5, 14, or 23

Your fiery, obstinate nature can sometimes make it difficult for you to accept suggestions or opinions from others, and your stubbornness may lead to quarrels or problems. You should be lucky with money and may often use your profits to set up new projects. Your innate intelligence will enable you to cope with a demanding career.

Day 6, 15, or 24

You have an open, stable, and cheerful character, and enjoy an active social life. You are affectionate and emotional, and have a tendency to daydream. This can lead to confusion, and your eagerness to help others may be stifled by your indecision. Although you will never be wealthy, you should always have enough money.

Day 7, 16, or 25

You enjoy a certain amount of excitement in your life, but must learn to become more realistic and disciplined. Although you are a natural performer, you should beware of alienating your friends or colleagues. In your career, the opportunity to travel is more important to you than a good salary or a high standard of living.

Day 8, 17, or 26

You have very good judgment, but should not act too quickly. Your social skills may sometimes be lacking, and you may alienate other people, so try to be more tactful. You will experience poverty, but also wealth. Your calm and determined nature is combined with a free spirit, making you best suited to self-employment.

Day 9, 18, or 27

You are happy, optimistic, and warmhearted. You keep yourself busy and are rarely troubled by trivialities. Occasionally you quarrel unnecessarily with your friends, and it is important for you to learn to control your moods. You are particularly suited to a career as a sole owner or proprietor.

YOUR CHINESE
HOUR OF BIRTH

In Chinese time, one hour is equal to two Western hours.
Each Chinese double hour is associated with one of the
twelve astrological animals.

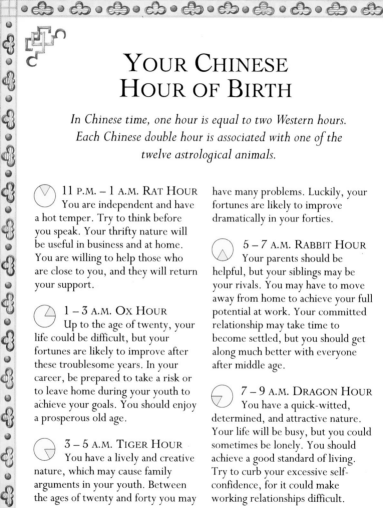

11 P.M. – 1 A.M. RAT HOUR
You are independent and have a hot temper. Try to think before you speak. Your thrifty nature will be useful in business and at home. You are willing to help those who are close to you, and they will return your support.

1 – 3 A.M. OX HOUR
Up to the age of twenty, your life could be difficult, but your fortunes are likely to improve after these troublesome years. In your career, be prepared to take a risk or to leave home during your youth to achieve your goals. You should enjoy a prosperous old age.

3 – 5 A.M. TIGER HOUR
You have a lively and creative nature, which may cause family arguments in your youth. Between the ages of twenty and forty you may have many problems. Luckily, your fortunes are likely to improve dramatically in your forties.

5 – 7 A.M. RABBIT HOUR
Your parents should be helpful, but your siblings may be your rivals. You may have to move away from home to achieve your full potential at work. Your committed relationship may take time to become settled, but you should get along much better with everyone after middle age.

7 – 9 A.M. DRAGON HOUR
You have a quick-witted, determined, and attractive nature. Your life will be busy, but you could sometimes be lonely. You should achieve a good standard of living. Try to curb your excessive self-confidence, for it could make working relationships difficult.

9 – 11 A.M. SNAKE HOUR

You have a talent for business and should find it easy to build your career and provide for your family. You have a very generous spirit and will gladly help your friends when they are in trouble. Unfortunately, family relationships are unlikely to run smoothly.

11 A.M. – 1 P.M. HORSE HOUR

You are active, clever, and obstinate. Try to listen to advice. You are fascinated with travel and with changing your life. Learn to control your extravagance, for it could lead to financial suffering.

1 – 3 P.M. RAM HOUR

Steady relationships with your family, friends, or partners are difficult, because you have an active nature. You are clever, but must not force your views on others. Your fortunes will be at their lowest in your middle age.

3 – 5 P.M. MONKEY HOUR

You earn and spend money easily. Your character is attractive, but frustrating, too. Sometimes your parents are not able to give you adequate moral support. Your committed relationship should be good, but do not brood over emotional problems for too long – if you do your career could suffer.

5 – 7 P.M. ROOSTER HOUR

In your teenage years you may have many arguments with your family. There could even be a family division, which should eventually be resolved. You are trustworthy, kind, and warmhearted, and never intend to hurt other people.

7 – 9 P.M. DOG HOUR

Your brave, capable, hard-working nature is ideally suited to self-employment, and the forecast for your career is excellent. Try to control your impatience and vanity. The quality of your life is far more important to you than the amount of money you have saved.

9 – 11 P.M. PIG HOUR

You are particularly skilled at manual work and always set yourself high standards. Although you are warmhearted, you do not like to surround yourself with too many friends. However, the people who are close to you have your complete trust. You can be easily upset by others, but are able to forgive and forget quickly.

YOUR FORTUNE IN OTHER ANIMAL YEARS

The Horse's fortunes fluctuate during the twelve animal years. It is best to concentrate on a year's positive aspects, and to take care when faced with the seemingly negative.

YEAR OF THE RAT
Trouble and strife are likely to make their presence felt in the Year of the Rat. You will feel quite pressured, and your family will be affected, too. However, if you are caring and considerate, events will eventually resolve themselves.

YEAR OF THE OX
To make the most of your opportunities, you will have to be fearless and brave. You will encounter difficulties in the Year of the Ox, but they can be turned to your advantage as long as you are bold enough to make sufficient effort.

YEAR OF THE TIGER
Your friends can be a positive guiding force, but they can also be troublesome and disruptive. Examine your friendships closely, and decide who is trustworthy and who you can easily do without.

YEAR OF THE RABBIT
You should enjoy considerable success in your professional life, financial affairs, and family life in the Year of the Rabbit. This year could prove to be one of the best of your life, but you must try to avoid petty quarrels and disagreements.

YEAR OF THE DRAGON
It is perhaps inevitable that this year will be an anticlimax after the successes of the last. Troubles are likely to loom in various areas of your life, and it may be beneficial to get away from your home environment for a while.

YEAR OF THE SNAKE

You must always stay on guard during the Year of the Snake. It would be very foolish to allow yourself to become involved in any speculative financial projects, and even old friends who offer you instant success should not be trusted.

YEAR OF THE HORSE

Many opportunities are available to you during this very good year. Seize these opportunities quickly, and do your best to make the most of them. Ill health could be a problem for you, but it should not curtail your potential for success.

YEAR OF THE RAM

You are not in any real danger this year, but it will be a time of considerable difficulty. Do not waste your energy by railing against your problems. It is best if you persevere quietly, and try to retain your integrity at all costs.

YEAR OF THE MONKEY

Energy and creativity are constantly flowing within you, making the Year of the Monkey a roaring success. This is no more than you deserve. Your own diligent efforts have created these opportunities, and you should continue to pursue them.

YEAR OF THE ROOSTER

You should be successful this year, but will have to cope with disruptive people. Try to keep your distance from them, for they will try to frustrate you and may even spoil your long-laid plans.

YEAR OF THE DOG

Good fortune will be yours during the Year of the Dog, but you should not allow yourself to become complacent. Study properly, plan sufficiently, and beware of minor disagreements that could escalate into serious conflict.

YEAR OF THE PIG

It is important that you take care of your health in the Year of the Pig. Ill health will create stress for you, causing you to hold yourself back in ventures when you should be making every effort to put yourself forward.

YOUR CHINESE
YEAR OF BIRTH

*Your astrological animal corresponds to the Chinese year of
your birth. It is the single most important key in the quest
to unlock your Chinese horoscope.*

Find your Western year of birth in
the left-hand column of the chart.
Your Chinese astrological animal is
on the same line as your year of birth
in the right-hand column of the
chart. If you were born in the
beginning of the year, check the

middle column of the chart carefully.
For example, if you were born in
1967, you might assume that you
belong to the Year of the Ram.
However, if your birthday falls
before February 9, you actually
belong to the Year of the Horse.

1900	Jan 31 – Feb 18, 1901	Rat
1901	Feb 19 – Feb 7, 1902	Ox
1902	Feb 8 – Jan 28, 1903	Tiger
1903	Jan 29 – Feb 15, 1904	Rabbit
1904	Feb 16 – Feb 3, 1905	Dragon
1905	Feb 4 – Jan 24, 1906	Snake
1906	Jan 25 – Feb 12, 1907	Horse
1907	Feb 13 – Feb 1, 1908	Ram
1908	Feb 2 – Jan 21, 1909	Monkey
1909	Jan 22 – Feb 9, 1910	Rooster
1910	Feb 10 – Jan 29, 1911	Dog
1911	Jan 30 – Feb 17, 1912	Pig
1912	Feb 18 – Feb 5, 1913	Rat
1913	Feb 6 – Jan 25, 1914	Ox
1914	Jan 26 – Feb 13, 1915	Tiger
1915	Feb 14 – Feb 2, 1916	Rabbit
1916	Feb 3 – Jan 22, 1917	Dragon

1917	Jan 23 – Feb 10, 1918	Snake
1918	Feb 11 – Jan 31, 1919	Horse
1919	Feb 1 – Feb 19, 1920	Ram
1920	Feb 20 – Feb 7, 1921	Monkey
1921	Feb 8 – Jan 27, 1922	Rooster
1922	Jan 28 – Feb 15, 1923	Dog
1923	Feb 16 – Feb 4, 1924	Pig
1924	Feb 5 – Jan 23, 1925	Rat
1925	Jan 24 – Feb 12, 1926	Ox
1926	Feb 13 – Feb 1, 1927	Tiger
1927	Feb 2 – Jan 22, 1928	Rabbit
1928	Jan 23 – Feb 9, 1929	Dragon
1929	Feb 10 – Jan 29, 1930	Snake
1930	Jan 30 – Feb 16, 1931	Horse
1931	Feb 17 – Feb 5, 1932	Ram
1932	Feb 6 – Jan 25, 1933	Monkey
1933	Jan 26 – Feb 13, 1934	Rooster

1934	Feb 14 – Feb 3, 1935	Dog	1971	Jan 27 – Feb 14, 1972	Pig
1935	Feb 4 – Jan 23, 1936	Pig	1972	Feb 15 – Feb 2, 1973	Rat
1936	Jan 24 – Feb 10, 1937	Rat	1973	Feb 3 – Jan 22, 1974	Ox
1937	Feb 11 – Jan 30, 1938	Ox	1974	Jan 23 – Feb 10, 1975	Tiger
1938	Jan 31 – Feb 18, 1939	Tiger	1975	Feb 11 – Jan 30, 1976	Rabbit
1939	Feb 19 – Feb 7, 1940	Rabbit	1976	Jan 31 – Feb 17, 1977	Dragon
1940	Feb 8 – Jan 26, 1941	Dragon	1977	Feb 18 – Feb 6, 1978	Snake
1941	Jan 27 – Feb 14, 1942	Snake	1978	Feb 7 – Jan 27, 1979	Horse
1942	Feb 15 – Feb 4, 1943	Horse	1979	Jan 28 – Feb 15, 1980	Ram
1943	Feb 5 – Jan 24, 1944	Ram	1980	Feb 16 – Feb 4, 1981	Monkey
1944	Jan 25 – Feb 12, 1945	Monkey	1981	Feb 5 – Jan 24, 1982	Rooster
1945	Feb 13 – Feb 1, 1946	Rooster	1982	Jan 25 – Feb 12, 1983	Dog
1946	Feb 2 – Jan 21, 1947	Dog	1983	Feb 13 – Feb 1, 1984	Pig
1947	Jan 22 – Feb 9, 1948	Pig	1984	Feb 2 – Feb 19, 1985	Rat
1948	Feb 10 – Jan 28, 1949	Rat	1985	Feb 20 – Feb 8, 1986	Ox
1949	Jan 29 – Feb 16, 1950	Ox	1986	Feb 9 – Jan 28, 1987	Tiger
1950	Feb 17 – Feb 5, 1951	Tiger	1987	Jan 29 – Feb 16, 1988	Rabbit
1951	Feb 6 – Jan 26, 1952	Rabbit	1988	Feb 17 – Feb 5, 1989	Dragon
1952	Jan 27 – Feb 13, 1953	Dragon	1989	Feb 6 – Jan 26, 1990	Snake
1953	Feb 14 – Feb 2, 1954	Snake	1990	Jan 27 – Feb 14, 1991	Horse
1954	Feb 3 – Jan 23, 1955	Horse	1991	Feb 15 – Feb 3, 1992	Ram
1955	Jan 24 – Feb 11, 1956	Ram	1992	Feb 4 – Jan 22, 1993	Monkey
1956	Feb 12 – Jan 30, 1957	Monkey	1993	Jan 23 – Feb 9, 1994	Rooster
1957	Jan 31 – Feb 17, 1958	Rooster	1994	Feb 10 – Jan 30, 1995	Dog
1958	Feb 18 – Feb 7, 1959	Dog	1995	Jan 31 – Feb 18, 1996	Pig
1959	Feb 8 – Jan 27, 1960	Pig	1996	Feb 19 – Feb 6, 1997	Rat
1960	Jan 28 – Feb 14, 1961	Rat	1997	Feb 7 – Jan 27, 1998	Ox
1961	Feb 15 – Feb 4, 1962	Ox	1998	Jan 28 – Feb 15, 1999	Tiger
1962	Feb 5 – Jan 24, 1963	Tiger	1999	Feb 16 – Feb 4, 2000	Rabbit
1963	Jan 25 – Feb 12, 1964	Rabbit	2000	Feb 5 – Jan 23, 2001	Dragon
1964	Feb 13 – Feb 1, 1965	Dragon	2001	Jan 24 – Feb 11, 2002	Snake
1965	Feb 2 – Jan 20, 1966	Snake	2002	Feb 12 – Jan 31, 2003	Horse
1966	Jan 21 – Feb 8, 1967	Horse	2003	Feb 1 – Jan 21, 2004	Ram
1967	Feb 9 – Jan 29, 1968	Ram	2004	Jan 22 – Feb 8, 2005	Monkey
1968	Jan 30 – Feb 16, 1969	Monkey	2005	Feb 9 – Jan 28, 2006	Rooster
1969	Feb 17 – Feb 5, 1970	Rooster	2006	Jan 29 – Feb 17, 2007	Dog
1970	Feb 6 – Jan 26, 1971	Dog	2007	Feb 18 – Feb 6, 2008	Pig

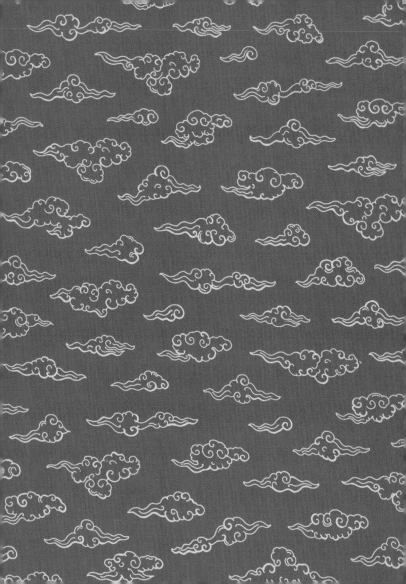